WAKING DREAMS

AND OTHER RHYMES

GAURAV BHATIA

Waking Dreams
and Other Rhymes

©2021 Gaurav Bhatia

First Edition

This book was professionally typeset on Reedsy.
Find out more at reedsy.com

WIZARD OF WORDS PUBLISHING L.L.C.
745 Barclay Cir
Unit 310
Rochester MI 48307

ISBN: 978-1-5136-8456-7

This book is dedicated to:

My wife, my daughters,

my parents...

....and to all my fellow dreamers

With all my love

– Gaurav Bhatia

May 2, 2021
Rochester, Michigan
The United States of America

CONTENTS

Amidst the Pandemic 2

Becoming Canadian 4

At the Gun Range 6

Midnight's Garden 10

Forever Young 12

Cheers 14

Waking Dreams 16

My Body, My Rules 18

Alternate Facts 20

Hope. 22

Religion 24

About Vacations 26

Break Free. 28

Regret 30

The Gates of Dachau 32

About Envy. 36

The Jaded 38

Being Human 40

Karma Bites 42

Mirror Mirror 44

AMIDST THE PANDEMIC

Trapped amidst the pandemic

as boredom turns endemic

an insufferable lockdown

the never ending countdown

now bathing every other day

refusing to shave, come what may

passing time with wistful sighs

silently becoming the Lord of the Flies

BECOMING CANADIAN

Rejoice, Your Majesty!
hire a jester, a circus, a singer
for you have acquired in your service
yet another trigger-happy finger
and even though this one happens to be brown
there shall be nary a blemish on your shiny crown
for to be forever faithful, I did take the oath
no matter how it made my colonial soul loath
oh how it made the heart fume and seethe
while I said the very words through gritted teeth
as I kept my mind focused on the prize
never once letting it escape my eyes
that piece of paper issued in your name
and even though I find monarchy, a concept lame
your passport is mighty, that much is true
what's a poor colonial to do?

if one wishes to travel the

world unchallenged, unfettered

to her Majesty's royal bosom

one must choose to remain tethered

AT THE GUN RANGE

My bored and tired mind
required some soothing
so I decided to try my hand
at clay shooting
off to the gun range I went
vowing not to return
until the last cartridge was spent

"Pull," I yelled, and
heaven bound, the disc surged
I pulled the trigger, but alas,
my aim and the target
they widely diverged
no matter if I launched
from points A, B, or C
the pellets missed their mark
by a wide degree

Consumed by self-loathing

and considerable disgust

I found that my aim, I could

no longer trust

I was indeed at the point

of utter dejection

when there came a moment

of self-reflection

I decided there could be no harm

in some innovation

perhaps all I lacked

was proper motivation

so imagining the discs to be

faces of foes, old and new,

I fired again, and presto!

my aim was no longer askew

as disc after disc

shattered to pieces

my self-esteem inched up

by radices

MIDNIGHT'S GARDEN

Many a dream are buried
in midnight's garden
alas, they couldn't see light of another day
hopes abandoned
hearts are hardened
and the smiles quietly tucked away

Dreams, akin to the morning flower
drunk on promise of eternal bloom
ever confident of their sun sun-kissed power
yet as approaches the midnight hour
the dreams turn from sweet, to sour
and thoughts turn to bitter gloom

The possibilities of daylight golden
die a slow death through the night
currency of dreams is hope eternal
fueling our souls, our very kernel
yet, worthless against the great nocturnal
best buried, without a fight

FOREVER YOUNG

Oh how the menage
wants me to act my age
an apt presage
to respectability
the persona dignified
at the cost of my soul
forever petrified

But what of my heart
that ever yearns
as it burns
for childish innocence
from whence wild dreams are sprung
thus keeping my heart free
and forever young?

CHEERS

In the garden of pious sobriety
one finds snakes of every variety
engaged in the usual blither
the slimy denizens slide and slither
sharing the same poison, bitter
fangs dripping with theocracy
unending coils of mobocracy
deadly in hypocrisy

In the garden of pious sobriety
I, the lone denizen
I carefully choose my poison
one made of grain, not venom
yet potent enough to benumb
thus I am able to not succumb
to the venom of my slithering peers
so becoming the sum of all their fears
I walk by, spreading bonhomie and cheers

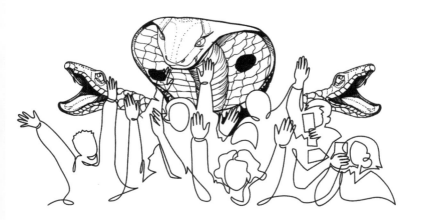

WAKING
DREAMS

Behold! A shooting star
makes its way, past the moon
but I can only admire from afar
though I'd follow, if I could

If one could change the nature of things
as absurd as it may sound
one could perhaps sprout some wings
and dare to follow the star around

Alas, earthbound I must remain
and shelve these absurd, unearthly schemes
however much the heart may strain
to follow the star, in waking dreams

MY BODY, MY RULES

Oh the farce! the distraction!
once again, the zealot faction
gets to revive the so-called fight
to snatch away a woman's
reproductive right

Oh imagine our acute frustration
that there is nary a legislation
put forth by an aspiring toady
to similarly seize control
over a man's body

ALTERNATE FACTS

If one ever wishes

to be taken for a fool

become the butt of jokes

and constant ridicule

to prove that common sense

has finally fled south

one needs to only

shut up with their mouth

instead, start talking

out of the ass

and take great pride

in bravado and sass

with which one must cover

the stinking pile of shite

as facts are butchered

in the dead of night

HOPE

Some people decide they can never win

they say for them, fate just has it in

so accepting a life of wistful sighing

they lay down their arms and give up trying

Alas, had they met the tiny ant

whilst bearing its burden up a slope

with neither complaint nor gripe or rant

they'd learn while there is life, there is hope

RELIGION

Religion is an impediment
to learn what's relevant
it's simply an embodiment
of self-serving rules

It's a tool to keep united
and perpetually ignited
those who prefer
the company of fools

Religion is an aberration
an unproven illation
it's simply oppression
in mystery swathed

It's a senseless oblation
to gods of our creation
often confused
with matters of faith

ABOUT
VACATIONS

Vacation with the family
that's no vacation
simply a change of location
where they have fun in the waves while
you remain stranded on the beach
like a crustacean
still tethered to your vocation
watching time pass, slower than ablation

Vacation with friends
now that's a real vacation
no matter what the location
days filled up with frolic
nights replete with drunken rollick
no sign of the erstwhile workaholic
a novel sensation
as time passes entirely too quickly
and thus we return with heightened conation

BREAK FREE

Follow your dreams

for they shall take you

to places you always

wanted to go

Follow your heart

for it will teach you

things that you always

wanted to know

If you can only muster the courage

to always do what you know is right

then conviction shall forever light your way

no matter how dark lies the night

If you can only find the strength

to break free from bonds of your making

there lies in wait, a whole new world

that is yours, just for the taking

REGRET

We live our lives

as willing fools

following a basket full of rules

restrictions bursting from the seams

constricting our very dreams

the important thing we tend to forget

burdened as we are with guilt and shame

when the curtain falls, there shall only be regret

for in the end, it's all the same

THE GATES OF DACHAU

The Gates of Dachau stand open
with an inscription for all to see
a dark and cruel token
"work sets you free"

Can you hear the ghostly echoes
of pitiful sobs and screams?
ringing across the ghettos
amongst the fields of green

See those dreadful towers
whence the wolves keep watch on sheep
that toil amongst the flowers
digging graves six feet deep

Feel the ground tremble
as the jackboots come marching
see the hopes crumble
when the death's heads come charging

The Gates of Dachau stand open
yawning darkness lies within
where many lives are broken
in this pit of despair and sin

Watch as families are torn apart
husband from wife, mother from child
genocide perfected to an art
in this place most defiled

Behold the silent progression
as the bakers are led to the oven
their only crime is their yarmulke
victims of an unholy coven

Behold the silent audience
that witness this circus of death
their only crime is their silence
as humanity takes its dying breath

The Gates of Dachau stand open
its walls a monument to infâme
where never a word was spoken
and heads now hang in shame

ABOUT ENVY

I often wonder of the reason, for envy having no
fixed season, 'tis present the year round

its influence is widely ranging, never waning, never
changing, such persistence does astound

Well known is the figment, of envy having certain
pigment, viridescent belike

Yet envy is far from visible, ever drawn to divisible,
ensnaring friend and foe alike

It'd be a glaring omission if envy was mistaken for
ambition, for the two could not have more differed

Of success, envy is contemptuous, yet of its fruits
'tis covetous, dismissing the sacrifices incurred

Dear Friend, do heed my warning, beware of those
given to fawning, while barely holding their bile

For indeed there is something slithering,
something churning, something withering,
hidden beneath that smile

THE JADED

Soul, oh soul come back to me!
for you should have never left my shell
and allowed me to fill it instead
with shiny, sordid gifts of hell

I sought to shake the devil's hand
in name of the greater good
to the detriment of my fellow man
I abandoned that for what I stood

Lately when I look in the mirror
it's a stranger who looks back at me
a cruel face with jaded eyes
devoid of all humanity

Soul, oh soul come back to me!
and bring with you the innocence of youth
the ignorance of lofty ideals
now marred forever by squalid truth

BEING HUMAN

Life in totality
is a journey all too brief
with an ever looming finality
so why the drama and grief
over my frail and fluid morality?

I have refused to follow
these rules of your making
knowing your promises to be hollow
their legitimacy was difficult to swallow
I knew the rules were for breaking

You have nothing with which to bind me
neither norm nor convention
shame does not blind me
for pride never confined me
with false hopes of ascension

I do not care if I exist
by divine will or happenstance
it is not society I resist
but loss of freedom and chance

to be human, just for once

KARMA BITES

God created man
presumably in his image
an effort vain that pays
to its maker, no homage
of God, man has no further use
divinity is relegated to the obtuse
for science has heavens in its sights
Karma bites

Man created intelligence
presumably in his image
albeit artificial
a notion farcical
the circle shall thus be complete
when intelligence deems men obsolete
and humanity falls from blinding heights
Karma bites

MIRROR MIRROR

Mirror Mirror on the wall
in a dusty old hall
with silvery strings adorned
dreaming of days bygone

Once sought by mighty kings
your mortal playthings
who blinded by greed and hate
failed to know the evil at their gate

Now covered with dust and pollen
how the once mighty have fallen
shattered by time's relentless flacks
forever marred by unsightly cracks

Mirror Mirror on the wall
in a dusty old hall
gone are the heady days of power
evil shall often self devour

ABOUT THE AUTHOR

Gaurav Bhatia is a Canadian author, information technology whiz, serial entrepreneur and self-styled comedian. His work across multiple themes broadly addresses narratives of the human experience.

Gaurav has a panache for travel, aviation and all good things life has to offer. He loves to share his unique perspective on life through poetry.

Gaurav lives with his wife, two daughters and two dogs in Rochester, Michigan.

Lightning Source UK Ltd.
Milton Keynes UK
UKHW020720090621
385189UK00007B/74